ROLAND SCHIMMELPFENNIG

German writer Roland Schimmelpfennig has worked as a journalist, translator and dramaturg and is currently writer in residence at the Deutsches Schauspielhaus Hamburg.

Push Up (translated by Maja Zade) was first produced at the Royal Court Theatre Upstairs in February 2002. Other work for the theatre in English includes *Arabian Nights* (translated by David Tushingham) which performed at Soho Theatre, London in 2002, and *The Woman Before* (translated by David Tushingham), commissioned by the Royal Court Theatre in 2005 for a main-house production. German plays include *Vorher/Nachher, Die Arabische Nacht, Vor langer Zeit im Mai, MEZ, Keine Arbeit für die junge Frau im Frühlingskleid, Die Zwiefachen, Die ewige Maria, Fisch um Fisch,* and *Aus den Städten in die Wälder, Aus den Wäldern in die Städte.*

Radio includes: *Krieg der Wellen,* (Hessischer Rundfunk, nominee for Radio play of the year), *Die Taxiterroristin* (Südwestfunk), *Vorher/Nachher* (Hessischer Rundfunk), *Die Aufzeichnung* (Südwestfunk).

Translation includes: *The Glory of Living, Sling Blade, Penetrator.*

Other Modern Plays in Translation

Marcos Barbosa
ALMOST NOTHING /
    AT THE TABLE
tr. Mark O'Thomas

Mikhail Bulgakov
FLIGHT
tr. Ron Hutchinson

Anton Chekhov
THE CHERRY ORCHARD
THE SEAGULL
THREE SISTERS
UNCLE VANYA
tr. Stephen Mulrine

Nikolai Erdman
THE MANDATE
tr. Declan Donnellan

Ulises Rodríguez Febles
THE CONCERT /
    EL CONCIERTO
tr. William Gregory

David Gieselmann
MR KOLPERT
tr. David Tushingham

Nikolai Gogol
THE GOVERNMENT
    INSPECTOR
tr. Stephen Mulrine

Maxim Gorky
CHILDREN OF THE SUN
tr. Stephen Mulrine

Henrik Ibsen
AN ENEMY OF THE PEOPLE
tr. Arthur Miller
HEDDA GABLER
tr. Richard Eyre
A DOLL'S HOUSE
HEDDA GABLER
THE LADY FROM THE SEA
THE MASTER BUILDER
PEER GYNT
ROSMERSHOLM
tr. Kenneth McLeish

JOHN GABRIEL BORKMAN
GHOSTS
tr. Stephen Mulrine

Federico García Lorca
BLOOD WEDDING
tr. Tanya Ronder
THE HOUSE OF
    BERNARDA ALBA
tr. Rona Munro

Ludmila Petrushevskaya
CINZANO &
    SMIRNOVA'S BIRTHDAY
tr. Stephen Mulrine

Luigi Pirandello
NAKED
tr. Nicholas Wright
SIX CHARACTERS IN
    SEARCH OF AN AUTHOR
tr. Stephen Mulrine

The Presnyakov Brothers
PLAYING THE VICTIM
tr. Sasha Dugdale
TERRORISM
tr. Sasha Dugdale

Friedrich Schiller
DON CARLOS
tr. Mike Poulton

Vassily Sigarev
BLACK MILK
LADYBIRD
PLASTICINE
tr. Sasha Dugdale

August Strindberg
THE DANCE OF DEATH
tr. Stephen Mulrine
A DREAM PLAY
tr. Caryl Churchill
MISS JULIE
tr. Kenneth McLeish

Frank Wedekind
LULU
tr. Nicholas Wright

Roland Schimmelpfennig

PUSH UP

translated by Maja Zade

NICK HERN BOOKS

LONDON

www.nickhernbooks.co.uk

A Nick Hern Book

Push Up first published in Great Britain in 2002 as a paperback
original by Nick Hern Books, 14 Larden Road, London
W3 7ST, by arrangement with Fischer Verlag

Reprinted 2006 (twice), 2007 (twice), 2009, 2010, 2011, 2012

Typeset by Country Setting, Kingsdown, Kent CT14 8ES
Printed and bound in Great Britain by Mimeo Ltd, Huntingdon,
Cambridgeshire, PE29 6XX

A CIP catalogue record for this book is available from the
British Library

ISBN 978 1 85459 684 0

Push Up was first performed at the Royal Court Theatre Upstairs, London, on 8 February 2002. The cast in order of appearance was as follows:

HEINRICH	Peter Sproule
ANGELIKA	Sian Thomas
SABINE	Lucy Whybrow
ROBERT	David Tennant
PATRIZIA	Jaqueline Defferary
HANS	Robin Soans
FRANK	Nigel Lindsay
MARIA	Flaminia Cinque

Director   Ramin Gray
Designer / Lighting Designer   Rodney Grant
Sound Designer   Ian Dickinson

Characters

HEINRICH

ANGELIKA

SABINE

ROBERT

PATRIZIA

HANS

FRANK

MARIA

A.

HEINRICH. I work for a pretty big corporation. I sit on the ground floor, behind the glass pane in the lobby. Everyone that works in the building walks past me. The building is big, really big, sixteen floors, and next to me there are monitors transmitting pictures from the security cameras.

In the control room we work shifts, usually in twos. On the night shift we also do the round through the building. On the night round we check every room, we unlock and lock every single room. That takes time. The building is extensive, there is everything you would imagine: the executive floor, the meeting rooms that still smell of cigarettes at night, the sectors of the different departments and sub-departments, the administration offices, development, the creative rooms, the labs and the huge computer control room in the basement. That's where they save data from all over the world: data from the branches in the US, South Africa, India.

Next to the monitors for the security cameras is my own little TV. It's not really allowed but no one says anything. Not even Kramer, who lives with the woman who more or less owns the corporation. Kramer basically runs this place. I'm not really sure what she does. But when she walks past, I always turn it off.

Sometimes they even show our company's ad – in our ad a man in a park carries a woman over a huge puddle. Then there's a slogan and our logo.

Pause.

It's strange. It's like it's nicked from somewhere. In any case the ad's been on for over a year and it's time for a new ad: maybe something completely different – something that has more to do with me – or with our products. I mean – I don't get the connection.

We usually work shifts in twos. I'm often on duty with Maria. Maria sees the ad very differently. She likes the ad. But I'd like something with more action. I like action films. Or thrillers.

Maria and I talk a lot about the things we watch on TV while we're doing our shift. About the couples in the films for example. I mean: in real life it's just different. People don't just get together. It's rare that two people meet and then bang, they fall in love. It hardly ever happens. Or that a man in a park carries a woman over a huge puddle like in our ad. When does that happen? 'Right? Right?' I say and turn to Maria.'I mean just look at you and me. I don't carry you across any puddles either.' And then she laughs.

1.1.

A top executive's office. ANGELIKA *and* SABINE *are sitting facing each other.*

ANGELIKA. I'm glad you're here.

Short pause.

I'm pleased. I was very curious how you – I'm sorry you had to wait those ten minutes. I'm really very pleased.

SABINE. You don't have to reassure me. I'm not nervous.

ANGELIKA. There's no reason to be nervous.

SABINE. Yes, there is. But I'm not.

ANGELIKA. No? I am, a little.

SABINE. You?

ANGELIKA. Yes, certainly.

Pause.

SABINE. Spare me.

ANGELIKA. What?

SABINE. These pleasantries. We don't need to make small talk here.

ANGELIKA. Is that what I'm doing?

SABINE. We both know there's a conflict here.

ANGELIKA. Maybe we assess the – situation differently.

SABINE. You say you're pleased I'm here.

ANGELIKA. Yes –

SABINE. You say you're sorry I had to wait outside
    corridor with your secretary. But none of that's tr
    not sorry. To make someone wait for more than fiv
    is a subliminal act of aggression. You know that ver

    Pause.

ANGELIKA. Ok. I hope my secretary explained why you   to
    wait. I still had to –

SABINE. You're trying to establish a certain climate of
    conversation here. You're trying to establish an atmosphere of
    friendliness, helpfulness and warmth which is completely
    inappropriate. You say you're nervous although that's
    probably not true. You're only doing that to relax the
    situation.

    But the situation can't be relaxed. No matter how you 'assess
    the situation'. There are obviously two different interests at
    stake here, and they don't meet.

ANGELIKA. Just a moment. Hang on.

SABINE. No –

ANGELIKA. Yes –

SABINE. It's completely –

ANGELIKA. Stop.

SABINE. So far the whole course of this conversation –

ANGELIKA. Stop.

SABINE *stands up if she was sitting.* No –

ANGELIKA. Sabine!

    Short pause.

    Can we begin to talk now?

    Short pause.

SABINE. As you like. Go on.

1.2.

ANGELIKA. To throw the coffee in her face was a gaffe.
    A lapse in control. But she didn't deserve any better. That
    piece of shit didn't deserve any better.

She sat there and tried to make a statement by being impertinent. Tried to pretend. Wanted to show strength. Self-confidence. Fake, but it wasn't bad. In her stupid blue suit. She probably has four just like it hanging in her wardrobe. Tasteless but pretentious. And successful. She sat there and didn't touch the coffee. Upset because she had to wait outside for ten minutes.

Actually I knew when she walked in through the door. I just wanted to see her one last time. She was sitting facing me and I was surprised by her cheek. The unbelievable cheek to even ask for this appointment.

How does she do it? How did she manage to seduce him – looking like that? With that pitiful air of expert knowledge and ambition.

1.3.

ANGELIKA. You're twenty-eight. That makes you the youngest head of department in the whole corporation.

SABINE. I know.

ANGELIKA. I trust you completely. Even though you've only worked here for one and a half years. Without supervision.

SABINE. That's not true.

ANGELIKA. No?

SABINE. No. Kramer regularly co-ordinates the department work output with the demands, expectations and needs of the board. That means there's constant quality control.

ANGELIKA. Yes. Correct. The demands and needs of the board. How could I forget? He does that. Kramer. Are you happy with this procedure? Doesn't sound like it.

SABINE. I am.

ANGELIKA. Are you happy with Kramer?

SABINE. Yes. I –

ANGELIKA. You can be completely honest. The fact that I live with Kramer shouldn't stop you in any way.

SABINE. There's no friction between Kramer and me.

ANGELIKA. No friction. Good.

SABINE. I'd like to talk about you turning me down for –

ANGELIKA. Just a sec, just a sec. I just want us both to be up to speed. So there are no misunderstandings. After all we don't know each other.

SABINE. I hardly think that there's a –

Interrupts herself.

All right.

ANGELIKA. You did a degree in America and then worked for two companies that sent you to Japan, Korea and Taiwan. Today you have your own team of twenty people in-house, some of whom are twice your age, and you get the best results. Correct me if I'm wrong.

SABINE. No, no.

ANGELIKA. You're a highly qualified woman. Kramer says you're efficient, reliable and innovative. Very impressive. Very.

SABINE. Yes. And that's why I don't understand why you –

ANGELIKA. Yes, yes.

SABINE. What?

ANGELIKA. Yes I know – of course. Let's take it slowly. Coffee?

SABINE. No thanks.

ANGELIKA. You don't drink coffee?

SABINE. No thanks –

ANGELIKA. You're sure?

SABINE. No thanks.

Nonetheless, ANGELIKA *pours two cups.* SABINE *doesn't touch hers.*

Please –

Pause.

ANGELIKA. You think I just sit here and do what I feel like.

SABINE. Isn't that what you do?

ANGELIKA. No. Forget that.

SABINE. I wouldn't know how to.

ANGELIKA. Stop it.

SABINE. No –

ANGELIKA. Forget the old hierarchic structures. We're flexible and unorthodox. Like you. Quality wins. Don't you agree?

Short pause.

Then you're not being fair.

SABINE. Why are you telling me this? Why are you talking about the hierarchic structure of the economic miracle claiming that it doesn't exist any more. Of course it exists. Even if you offer me coffee. Even if you claim you trust me, which is obviously not true. I work for you. You decide what I do. So – let's not pretend.

ANGELIKA. Exactly.

SABINE. What?

ANGELIKA. I said: exactly. Let's not pretend. Good.

1.4.

SABINE. I haven't had sex in two years. And I'm twenty-eight. I get up at six every morning. I take a cold shower and then I have breakfast. Usually fruit. In my dressing gown. While I watch TV. I do that every morning except Sunday. In the morning I watch TV from half past six until seven. The programme's not very good at that time but I sit in front of the TV and think about nothing.

Then I start to get dressed. I never wear the same thing as the day before. Never. Although my clothes often look similar. I have many clothes. Heaps. I chose my apartment with this in mind. Built-in cupboards. In my current flat there are two built-in cupboards.

I can't decide what to wear. It's a problem. I often change my clothes completely several times over before I can decide what to wear. Until I've managed to make a decision. It's not easy. It's an ordeal.

When I'm dressed I blow-dry my hair and put on make-up. My hairstyle is okay, there's not much you can do with my hair. Make-up is difficult, especially in winter, when it's still dark outside. Not too much. Just high-quality products. From Japan for example.

Short pause.

When I've done my face I take the lift to the basement garage. It's eight o'clock now. Halfway down I stop and turn back. Go back up. Because I feel awful. I can't stand it. I can't stand it. I unlock the two safety locks to my apartment and get changed. I don't like what I'm wearing. I usually wear blue. I don't really like blue except maybe jeans or winter sweaters, but nonetheless I usually wear blue. I've taken to wearing everything in blue. To buy blue clothes when I have the time. Everything I buy is blue. So – everything's colour co-ordinated.

Nonetheless I turn around halfway down and get changed again. I change everything. My stockings, my knickers, my bra. I feel ugly. I have to hurry, the clock's ticking, and I'm standing in front of the mirror in the hall feeling ugly.

After a while it's gone half past eight. It's time, I need to go. Again I take the lift to the basement garage. Get into the car. I can't turn back now. To turn back now is completely impossible. I look in the rear-view mirror. My make-up is terrible. I don't like my lipstick. In the traffic jam on the circular I redo my lips. I can't do my eyes until I'm in the office. Whatever you do, don't look cheap.

I arrive at the office and I feel like no one's looking at me. That's good. That's awful.

At nine fifteen I see my team. None of the women at the long table wear blue. Except for when they wear jeans or winter sweaters maybe, but you don't see a lot of those here. In the meetings. Many of them are average. Very average. Most of them.

None of them wear blue.

Short pause.

I look into the faces at the table and I ask myself which of them had sex last night, and how often. Or this morning. While I took a cold shower. While I watched TV and thought about nothing.

All of them, I think. All of them except me.

1.5.

ANGELIKA. You climbed the ladder fast here. And of course you want to carry on climbing. I can understand that.

Short pause.

I was just like that. We're alike. Right?

SABINE. Maybe.

ANGELIKA. No, definitely.

SABINE. If you like.

ANGELIKA. We could be friends. No. We couldn't.

SABINE. Aha.

ANGELIKA. You could only pretend. Because you've got this hierarchical structure in your head and you want to be at the top of it.

SABINE. Whether we could be friends or not is not the point. This is about my qualifications, that's all. You're refusing to recognise them. This conversation is absurd.

ANGELIKA. Qualifications. Yes.

Short pause.

It's strange we haven't bumped into each other more often. Ever been up here, to the sixteenth floor?

SABINE. A couple of times.

ANGELIKA. That's all?

Short pause.

To Kramer's office I suppose.

SABINE. Exactly.

ANGELIKA. Do you like it up here?

SABINE. Of course. Are you making small talk again?

ANGELIKA. Exactly.

Pause.

You applied for the Delhi job.

SABINE. And you turned me down.

ANGELIKA. Yes.

SABINE. With no comment.

ANGELIKA. With no written comment.

SABINE. With no comment. With no explanation. No phonecall. Nothing. That's why I asked for an appointment.

ANGELIKA. Of course you did. After all you're the one that wants something.

SABINE. That means –

ANGELIKA. I knew you'd come.

SABINE. But you're not giving me any answers.

ANGELIKA. I will in a minute. I just wanted to get to know you a bit better first.

Short pause.

Our Delhi branch is the heart of our development department.

SABINE. I gave some important input in the development area. Decisive input. I don't want you to do me a favour. You should put me in the position where I can be of most use to the company. In Delhi.

ANGELIKA. But I've no intention of sending you to Delhi.

SABINE. Why?

ANGELIKA. You don't care about serving the company. No one is asking that either. You care about getting ahead, Sabine. That's understandable.

Short pause.

The thing I don't like is your method.

SABINE. My method is highly effective, as you already said. The benefits for the company are self-evident.

ANGELIKA. If I give you this job you'll end up at the head of this corporation. Sooner or later you'll end up on the board. Because with the know-how you're going to acquire in Delhi you'll become indispensable to us.

SABINE. That's true of every person you give this job to. The way I see things, there can only be two reasons why you don't trust me: one – my age, and two – my sex.

Didn't you just say that the old hierarchical structures don't exist any more?

ANGELIKA. Yes, yes. Sure.

Short pause.

But what if my own employees are taking advantage of those mechanisms?

SABINE. I don't know what you mean.

ANGELIKA. I mean exactly what I just said: but what if my own employees are taking advantage of those mechanisms.

SABINE. Who do you mean?

ANGELIKA. You.

SABINE. Me?

ANGELIKA. Yes, you.

SABINE. I have no idea what you're talking about.

ANGELIKA. No?

SABINE. No.

ANGELIKA. Kramer recommended I send you to Delhi.

SABINE. Yes?

ANGELIKA. Yes.

SABINE. Then why don't you give me the job.

ANGELIKA. No.

SABINE. You can't fault my qualifications.

ANGELIKA. Maybe not.

SABINE. But –

ANGELIKA. But you won't get the job.

SABINE. Why not?

ANGELIKA. Because Kramer recommended you.

SABINE. I see –

ANGELIKA. Yes.

Pause.

SABINE. You're living with Kramer. What's wrong with a recommendation from Kramer?

ANGELIKA *hesitates.* Kramer.

SABINE. I want the job. There's no one that could do a better job.

ANGELIKA. Says who?

SABINE. Says I. Says Kramer. Consider my application.

ANGELIKA *laughs*. I thought you said: consider my menstruation.

SABINE. What?

ANGELIKA. Nothing.

1.6.

ANGELIKA. My husband doesn't sleep with me anymore. Kramer. I'm XX years old.

I get up at six every morning. I take a cold shower and then I have breakfast. Usually fruit. At the kitchen counter. In my dressing gown. With a towel round my head and slippers on my feet. So I don't get cold and end up ill. While I eat I watch the small TV in our kitchen. I do that every morning except Sunday and sometimes Saturday. In the morning I watch TV from half past six until seven. The programme's not very good at that time, but I sit in front of the TV and think about nothing. That's nice. Then I start to get dressed and put on make-up. I never wear the same thing as the day before. Never. It used to take me a long time to decide what to wear. Every morning getting dressed was an ordeal. It still takes a long time, but before I didn't even know what to wear –

Today I simply go shopping more often. That doesn't really solve the problem but it helps. At least temporarily. When I don't know what to wear anymore I go shopping. Or I have them send me things. But mostly I go shopping because I need someone to help me. A shop assistant. Advice. I ask the shop assistants what suits me or what they'd recommend. I sort of let the shop assistants dress me, and sometimes that works. Often it doesn't.

The good thing about expensive shops is that the shop assistants there often have better taste than in the cheap ones. Not always, though.

It's not even as if I don't notice that the shop assistant has bad taste. I don't know how I can tell. Maybe from the eyes. Or the hair. Or the teeth.

When I go shopping I buy a lot. I never look for a single item. When I go shopping I look for a complete new wardrobe.

Skirts. Blouses. Suits. Jeans, which I'm really too fat to wear
– or imagine I'm too fat to wear, as the shop assistant tells
me. Dresses, shoes. Scarves. Belts. Absurd stuff.

My shopping trip gives me confidence. The confidence that I
can buy things, that I can have things I really need.

Every two months I give away two bags full of clothes. I take
them to the Red Cross shop. Or I give the clothes to my
neighbours' two daughters. But of course they don't fit. They
only take them because they're polite. I often put clothes I've
never worn in these bags. Clothes that I knew I'd never wear
when I bought them. Sometimes. That I put in the wardrobe
in the evening so I could wear them the next day. And then I
didn't like them in the morning. Because they didn't go with
anything. Mint green sweaters. Golden summer sandals. But
suddenly I didn't own a skirt to go with them. Double-
breasted jackets with shoulder pads. Silver lurex sweaters for
cocktail parties.

Those are slips. Lapses in control. Those are states of
emergency. But you can never tell that at the time.

Years ago someone advised me to buy everything in one
colour. Because that makes it easier to match clothes. But
what colour suits me. I can't decide that, can I.

So I wear something that I give away to the Red Cross in two
months' time at most. And then I blow-dry my hair and start
to put on make-up. It's about eight o'clock. Kramer gets up
and disappears to the shower in his private bathroom.

My hairstyle is okay, there's not much you can do with my
hair. Make-up is difficult, especially when it's still dark
outside. Not too much. Just the minimum required. Just high-
quality products. From Japan for example.

Short pause.

I arrive at the office around nine o'clock, Kramer at my side,
that's the rule. Everyone looks at me. No one looks me in the
eye but everyone looks at me. Years ago I thought I was
imagining things. That's what Kramer says for example. But
that's not true. That's awful.

At nine thirty I have my first meeting. In front of me are a
bunch of freshly shaved men. In suits I already know. Very
average. Most of them.

Short pause.

I wonder if they're wondering when I last had sex. I once told Kramer. Years ago. A couple of years ago, when things were still different.

1.7.

ANGELIKA. Do you think I'm attractive?

SABINE. Do you want an honest answer?

ANGELIKA *hesitates, smiles.* No.

SABINE. I think you're attractive.

ANGELIKA. Would you say that Kramer thinks I'm attractive?

SABINE. I can't say.

ANGELIKA. Do you think Kramer is attractive?

SABINE. Kramer is good-looking.

ANGELIKA. I think so too.

Short pause.

Does Kramer think you're attractive?

SABINE. You'd have to ask Kramer.

ANGELIKA. I don't think you're particularly attractive.

SABINE. Aha.

ANGELIKA. But I don't think I'm particularly attractive either. Like I said: we're alike.

Great at our jobs but looks-wise very average.

Granted, you're younger. If we were friends, Sabine, we'd only have to look at each other in the morning and we'd smile. Because both of us would know how long the other had stood in front of the mirror in the morning, desperately applying eye shadow. Trying to make her boring face more interesting.

Like billions of other women. Like all the cashiers in supermarkets and secretaries in offices. Strange, isn't it? Just think how much time and money is spent on that all over the world – what a waste.

If we were friends we'd know these things about each other. We could look each other in the eye, the carefully made-up eye, and laugh. About us. About our desperate struggle in front of the mirror in the morning.

The two women look at each other in silence for a long, long time.

SABINE. I don't know what you're trying to get at.

ANGELIKA. But you know why you're here.

SABINE. Yes. I'm the one that asked for this appointment.

Short pause.

ANGELIKA. And do you also know why you got this appointment?

SABINE. I have a right to –

ANGELIKA. Because Kramer recommended you.

SABINE. Yes, I know.

ANGELIKA. He says the Indians are too fast for the others.

SABINE. I'm fast.

ANGELIKA. I know. I know how fast you are. You have a sharp analytical mind. You spot the flaw in the system.

SABINE. That's my job.

ANGELIKA. Right.

Short pause.

But that doesn't mean you have to take the piss.

SABINE. I'm not taking the piss.

ANGELIKA. Hello. Sabine. You fucking are.

Pause.

You've only been here for a year and a half. Kramer wants to give you Delhi. Do you know what that means?

SABINE. You tell me.

ANGELIKA. That means Kramer has fucked you, Sabine.

Pause. Malicious:

He's fucked you. And maybe he's still fucking you. Is he still fucking you?

Silence.

SABINE. Yes.

Pause.

ANGELIKA. I expected you to deny that.

SABINE. Really?

ANGELIKA. And that's why he's sending you to Delhi. As a small thank you for fucking him.

SABINE. I don't think so.

ANGELIKA. When was the last time?

SABINE. What?

ANGELIKA. When was the last time he fucked you?

Short pause.

SABINE. About two hours ago. Downstairs in my office.

ANGELIKA. Good. The last time he fucked me was last night. In our mutual living room.

SABINE *smiles.* Then we do share a tragic fate after all.

Short pause.

Why don't you just throw me out?

ANGELIKA. By the way: I really did try to establish an atmosphere of objectivity, friendliness and professional behaviour. I tried. You didn't.

Just so you understand: the problem is not that you're fucking my husband. The problem is that you need to.

Suddenly.

That you're not good enough. Who knows how you managed to come this far – who you gave blow jobs in lifts in – where was it? Japan, Korea and Taiwan.

Maybe that's your talent. Maybe that's your true calling. It's just that we don't need someone like that in Delhi – a woman that intends to fuck her way to the top.

She collects herself.

That a woman with your education, with your so-called qualifications, as you put it, thinks she can get to the top like that is just pathetic.

But that you try to pull that stunt in my office, with my husband, is almost an insult. How stupid do you think I am? It's not on, Sabine.

But why am I telling you this? You already know that. You're the one with the sharp analytical mind. And that's why you'll go back to the fourth floor and clear out your office. You stupid piece of shit. You stupid, stupid piece of shit.

She throws her coffee in SABINE's *face.*

1.8.

SABINE. Of course there was never anything between me and her husband. Absolutely unthinkable. My relationship with Kramer was a purely professional one. He valued me as an employee but he wasn't interested in me or my tits. He never had been. If he had I would have gone to bed with him. At once.

But it was nice that she thought I had fucked him. It was nice how convinced she was. That she thought me capable of it.

I walked down the corridor to the lift with the coffee in my face and hair and on the blue suit. There are four just like it hanging in my wardrobe. Petra, the secretary, looked at me with a stupid expression on her face.

But she looked at me.

I left the office door open, which I would never have done normally. I waited in front of the lift and felt the coffee running down my neck. I stared at the lit button next to the lift door and heard a noise coming from her office.

Phrases I had heard on TV that morning came into my mind. I could hear the announcer's voice. I could see her in front of me, and her suit.

Kramer came out of his office and walked past me. Didn't say hello. He probably didn't even see me. I'm sure he didn't. Otherwise he would have asked – and then the lift arrived.

ANGELIKA. I stayed behind my desk. She walked out and left the door open. Cheap. I knew I'd never see her again. She'd go down to the fourth floor and clear her space. And piss off.

I sat there and couldn't concentrate. Phrases I had heard on TV that morning came into my mind. I could hear the announcer's voice. I could see her in front of me, and her suit.

Suddenly I felt like there was a hair down my throat. A long hair that went all the way down my gullet. I tried to swallow it but it didn't budge. I was nearly sick. I tried to get it out with my fingers, but I couldn't reach it. I put almost my entire hand in my mouth, but I couldn't reach it. And I made a choking sound and tried to suppress it because the door was still open. I felt the sweat running down my neck. Outside I could hear steps, the lift doors opened. Kramer put his head into my office and said everything ok, darling? Yes, I said, yes, yes, sure, everything ok.

B.

Indian music. Early morning: it's 5.45 a.m. HEINRICH *puts his bag down and opens his locker. He takes off his coat and puts it into the locker. He takes off his shoes, his sweater and his trousers, folds them carefully and puts them away. Then he takes out his uniform and puts it on. Finally he puts his shoes back on, takes his bag and pulls out a few things he's going to need throughout the day. He's still got time. As usual he's going to take over from his colleagues doing the night shift at five to six.*

2.1.

ROBERT *and* PATRIZIA. *In Robert's office. Both are in their early thirties. He's sitting behind his desk. She's sitting in front of it. He's holding a stack of paper in his hands, he is reading. There's a loaded, aggressive silence. Pause. He turns over a page, carries on reading. Finally:*

ROBERT. No way.

Short pause.

PATRIZIA. What?

ROBERT. You heard me: no way.

Short pause.

PATRIZIA. That –

ROBERT. You can forget it.

PATRIZIA. I don't understand –

ROBERT. It's very simple –

PATRIZIA. Hang on, why –

ROBERT. That –

PATRIZIA. I can –

ROBERT. Yes –

PATRIZIA. I can't –

ROBERT. Yes you can.

PATRIZIA. I certainly can't –

ROBERT. Yes you can –

PATRIZIA. No –

ROBERT. You can forget it. Forget it.

Short pause.

PATRIZIA. What is that supposed to mean: –

Short pause

ROBERT. What is that supposed to mean?

PATRIZIA. Yes –

ROBERT. What is that supposed to mean?

PATRIZIA. That was the question, that was my question, yes –

ROBERT. It's obvious isn't it: it means that you can –

PATRIZIA. Obvious? Nothing's obvious. There's nothing that's obvious here. Nothing at all. There's nothing that appears to be obvious here.

ROBERT. This paper –

PATRIZIA. This paper is –

ROBERT. This paper is not –

PATRIZIA. This paper is my –

ROBERT. This paper is not acceptable.

PATRIZIA. Not acceptable?

ROBERT. Not ac-cept-able. No way. You can't do this. That's that.

PATRIZIA. What?

ROBERT. Yes –

PATRIZIA. Have you gone –

ROBERT. This paper –

PATRIZIA. This paper –

ROBERT. This paper is zilch. Zilch.

Short pause.

PATRIZIA. It's zilch.

Short pause.

ROBERT. Yes.

PATRIZIA. It's not acceptable.

ROBERT. That's right.

Short pause.

PATRIZIA. Not acceptable.

ROBERT. Exactly.

Pause.

PATRIZIA. You're sick, Robert.

Short pause.

You're completely sick.

Short pause.

You're not serious.

ROBERT. I'm completely serious.

PATRIZIA. Rubbish. It's in your own interest to –

ROBERT. I'm completely serious. This paper is zilch. This paper is not worth talking about.

PATRIZIA. This paper is my outline and I have no idea why the two of us would have to talk about it.

ROBERT. I don't care. This thing is not going to get past my desk, you can be absolutely sure of that.

PATRIZIA. This thing is my new outline, and if you don't pass it on to Kramer then –

ROBERT. Excuse me, Excuse me –

PATRIZIA. No. If you don't pass it on to Kramer then I'm going
    to –

ROBERT. Did you just say 'new'? 'Your new outline'?

PATRIZIA. Yes, it's my new outline –

ROBERT. But this outline, Patrizia, is not new.

Short pause.

PATRIZIA. Pardon?

ROBERT. This outline is not new.

PATRIZIA. What?

ROBERT. This outline is old, Patrizia. Old.

Short pause.

This outline is old. Old, old, old.

2.2.

PATRIZIA. It was the best sex I've ever had.

Short pause.

Our eyes met and we both knew it was going to happen. I
sensed that he sensed it and he sensed that I sensed it. We
looked at each other across the room and we knew. Bang.

A party on the sixteenth floor. The executive floor. The party
was in full swing. Kramer had made a speech. They were
popping corks. There was laughter in the room, soft music,
discreet lights. Like in a film.

I'm wearing a short dress.

He's clinking glasses with a woman, but I know he's
watching me. He's in his early thirties. I've heard a lot about
him but we've never been introduced. He's successful. He's a
whiz kid, he works closely with Kramer: the stuff that
reaches Kramer goes past his desk first. Ambitious,
enthusiastic, you can tell. The world is his oyster: as long as
he doesn't let Kramer down there's a bright future ahead of
him.

The sound of many voices, the chinking of glasses, laughter.
Behind the windows, below us, is the city and the night.

I get a refill and walk to the door. Slowly, without turning around. I walk down the corridor. Silently, because my stilettos don't make a sound on the thick carpet. In my left hand I'm holding the glass of champagne, and with my right index finger I'm tracing the corridor wall. I turn the doorknobs. Most of the offices are locked. Kramer's office is open.

2.3.

PATRIZIA *and* ROBERT *in Robert's office.*

ROBERT. This outline is old.

PATRIZIA. The idea is new.

ROBERT. This is absurd.

PATRIZIA. Absurd?

ROBERT. Absurd, yes.

PATRIZIA. This is not absurd –

   Short pause

   This is the outline for my new ad.

ROBERT. Ok, ok, ok. The outline is new.

   Pause.

   The outline is new,

   Short pause

   But the ad is old. Right?

PATRIZIA. Maybe you can't read.

   Short pause.

ROBERT. This ad is identical to the last ad.

PATRIZIA. Pardon?

   Short pause.

ROBERT. It's identical to the last ad.

PATRIZIA. I don't believe this.

ROBERT. – and you of all people should know that.

PATRIZIA. I don't know what you mean.

ROBERT *throws the stack of paper on his desk.* Yes you do, yes, you do.

PATRIZIA. Oh really?

ROBERT. You certainly do. Of course you know that, Patrizia.

PATRIZIA. You're talking bollocks. I haven't got the faintest clue what you're talking about.

Short pause.

And you obviously don't either.

Short pause.

ROBERT. Forget about this outline. Your new ad and your old ad are identical.

PATRIZIA. This is bordering on insanity.

ROBERT. The only difference is the cost.

PATRIZIA. It's obviously completely insane to discuss it with you. A complete waste of time.

ROBERT. Twenty times the cost for the same product – you must have overlooked that. We really don't need to discuss it. It's insane. It's sick. Or just stupid.

Pause.

It's not good enough and I'm not going to pass it on to Kramer. Not with me, Patsy, forget it.

PATRIZIA. Fuck you. Fuck you, Robert.

Short pause.

And don't call me Patsy.

2.4.

ROBERT. It was the best sex I've ever had.

Short pause.

Kramer was throwing a party on the sixteenth floor. Everyone was there. They were popping champagne corks. Everyone in high spirits. The view from the windows onto the city lights and the night. Almost like in a film. Everything was going well. Soft music in the background. Kramer was in a good mood. Despite the India thing.

Short pause.

She looked totally adorable, breathtaking. She was wearing a short dark dress. Our eyes met as soon as she walked in the room. We looked at each other and we knew. She knew. I knew. It was obvious. Of course I'd heard a lot about her. But we had never been introduced.

Short pause.

The ad with the puddle was her idea. Her project. And her success. In the space of twelve months the puddle helped her rise to the top of her department.

Short pause.

The puddle ad was our breakthrough. It was a stock phrase: the puddle. Patrizia's ad with the puddle. Or else: Patsy's puddle ad. Everyone calls her Patsy.

Short pause.

The puddle was almost a legend.

Short pause.

Kramer's wife is clinking glasses with me but I don't let Patrizia out of my sight for more than a couple of seconds. She's standing at the opposite end of the room.

I watch how she's moving, how the light caresses her shoulders. I know that she knows that I'm watching her while I'm talking to Kramer's wife –

Even if she doesn't look over.

She gets a refill and walks to the door. Where is she going? She's holding the glass in her left hand.

Short pause.

I give her twenty seconds exactly, then I excuse myself and follow her.

I catch sight of her just as she's disappearing into Kramer's office. I walk along the corridor. You can't hear my steps on the carpet. The door to Kramer's office is ajar.

2.5.

In Robert's office. PATRIZIA *and* ROBERT.

PATRIZIA. Fuck you. Fuck you, Robert.

Short pause.

And don't call me Patsy.

ROBERT. What?

PATRIZIA. Patsy. You just said Patsy. Instead of Patrizia.

ROBERT. Oh right, that's possible.

PATRIZIA. To change another person's name suggests a more or less conscious intention to dominate her.

ROBERT *not interested.* Aha –

PATRIZIA. If you don't call me by my name that means you don't accept me for what I am. That you'd like me to be different: perhaps somehow more manageable.

Pause.

But that's not going to happen, Robert.

Pause.

The problem is not that the old and the new ads are similar. The problem is that you're too dumb to recognise the difference.

ROBERT. Correct. Because there isn't one.

Pause.

PATRIZIA. The new ad is set in Central Park.

Short pause.

ROBERT. And?

PATRIZIA. And what? That's the point.

Short pause.

ROBERT. The new ad is set in Central Park. The last ad was set in some park or other. What's different about Central Park?

Pause.

PATRIZIA. The light.

ROBERT. Oh.

PATRIZIA. Central Park is in New York. – In the United States of America.

ROBERT. Right. America, New York. Yes. Central Park is in New York.

PATRIZIA. There you go –

ROBERT. And what else? A park, grass, a path. A puddle, a man, a woman.

Short pause.

It's all identical. Identical.

PATRIZIA. A park, grass, a path. A puddle, a man, a woman.

Short pause.

Did I get that right?

ROBERT. Absolutely right.

Pause.

PATRIZIA. You forgot something.

ROBERT. A park, grass, a path. A puddle, a man, a woman.

He thinks.

Squirrel. The squirrel is new.

Short pause.

PATRIZIA. Wrong.

ROBERT *laughs*. Wrong? Aha. Well. Maybe I really have missed an important detail.

PATRIZIA. Autumn. September. The trees. The skyline. You forgot the skyline.

ROBERT. The skyline – right, the skyline. That's also in the –

Short pause.

– outline.

PATRIZIA. The New York skyline.

ROBERT. The skyline – interesting. A man, a woman, a puddle, a skyline. Respect.

Short pause.

Not to forget the squirrel, sorry. The squirrel in autumn in front of the skyline. That's why we need the –

Short pause

– the New York animal trainer.

PATRIZIA. The New York skyline is crucial.

ROBERT. The New York skyline is a load of shit.

2.6.

PATRIZIA. I glide into Kramer's office and leave the door ajar.
I'm standing in the dark in the strange office by the window
and I look at the city lights. If Kramer walks in now I'll
probably get fired. On the spot. I've no right to be in
Kramer's office, it's wrong.

Behind my back the door opens – I can tell from the yellow
streaks of light on the carpet – and it closes again, but I don't
turn around. He doesn't turn the light on. He stands right
behind me, I can feel his breath. I know it's him. I know it.
He puts his hands round my waist. He turns me and we kiss.
He pushes me against the window pane and pulls up my
dress.

We have sex. Unbelievably passionate sex.

Short pause.

And afterwards we went back to the party – we didn't even
speak to each other – and mingled. As planned. But we
hadn't planned it.

Short pause.

We hadn't planned anything. I meant to call him the next day
in his office, but –

Short pause.

I didn't call him. Not because I didn't want to call him, of
course I wanted to call him, but I thought: it's better if he
calls. In general I don't have a problem with making the first
move – I mean –

Short pause.

– either at work or with men. But – this was something else.
There was more at stake here.

This was –

Short pause.

This was too important.

Short pause.

And that's why I couldn't call him. It wouldn't have felt right. It would have been a serious mistake, I'm still completely sure of that.

I didn't want him to think I needed to call. That I felt the slightest need to call.

There was no reason to make him think that he could have me. It was about making it clear to him that I'm like him. Like him, in the same league, just in a different area. Creative, hard-working. Tough if I have to be.

Even now, in my early thirties, I have a job others will never get in their entire careers.

We were so alike – we simply belonged together. And that's why I didn't call him.

Short pause.

But I tried to bump into him, more or less by chance. I looked for him – in the car park, in the lobby, by the lifts, in the canteen or after work in one of the little Italian restaurants round the corner. Where everyone always goes.

Short pause.

I tried to find out when he arrived for work and when he finished, but I never bumped into him. And he didn't get in touch.

Short pause.

He probably thought of me as a fling. Maybe he did that kind of thing all the time. He probably didn't give a damn about me. I bet he didn't even think about it anymore.

Short pause.

I got angry.

Short pause.

I got angry because he didn't realise who he was dealing with. He didn't call. He didn't think I was worth it. And I was going to punish him for that. No, not punish – destroy. I wanted to ruin him. Ruin.

Short pause.

Nonetheless I kept on looking for him: in the lobby, in the car park, in the canteen, in the little Italian restaurants round the corner. But he wasn't there.

Short pause.

And then Kramer came up to me and said it was time for a new ad: and had I ever met his right hand man, Robert.

Kramer said I should get in touch with Robert about the new ad. It was bound to be interesting for both of us.

2.7.

ROBERT. It's dark in Kramer's office. She's standing with her back towards me, by the window.

I'm right behind her. She smells just like I imagined. If Kramer walks in now and finds us in his office we'll both get fired. On the spot.

I put my hands round her waist and turn her. We kiss. I push her against the window and pull up her dress. We have sex. Incredible, passionate sex.

Pause.

Afterwards we go back to the party and mingle, and Kramer says: Robert, I was about to look for you –

Short pause.

Of course I was going to call her the next day. But –

Short pause.

– but then I didn't. I wanted to – but I didn't. Although in my job I often make the first move, I don't have a problem with that – in general. Either at work or –

Short pause.

– in my private life.

But – but this, this was different. This was something else. This was not just a fling. There was more at stake here. This was big.

This woman was important. This woman was spectacular –

Short pause.

You can't just call a woman like that. It would have been a mistake, I'm still certain of that. I didn't want her to think I needed to get in touch with her.

We were in the same league, we just worked in different areas: we were both competent, flexible, innovative and hard on ourselves and on others. Even now, in our early thirties, we had jobs others will never manage to get. She didn't have one up on me and I didn't have one up on her. She was like me: I was like her, and I wanted her to know that. We – her and me – we belonged together.

And that's why I couldn't call her.

Short pause.

But I tried to bump into her. In the car park or in the lobby by the lifts. Or in the canteen or in one of the little Italian restaurants round the corner. But I didn't find her. I looked for her, I tried to find out when she arrived for work in the morning and when she left, but it didn't work.

Short pause.

And she didn't call. She didn't get in touch. No phone call, no note. Maybe for her I was just a fling in her boss's office. She wasn't interested in me. She didn't get in touch. Maybe she thought I wasn't worth it.

She didn't give a damn about me.

Short pause.

Gradually I got angry. I got angry because she didn't call me.

Short pause.

I got angry because she didn't realise who she was dealing with, what we could have been together. I meant nothing to her, and she was going to pay for that. One day I was going to really make her pay for that.

Short pause.

Nonetheless I kept on looking for her: in the car park, in the lobby, in front of the lifts, and in the canteen and after work in the little restaurants and bars round the corner. And then Kramer came up to me and said it was time for a new ad. Had I ever met Patrizia – and that I should get in touch with her. It was bound to be interesting for both of us.

2.8.

In Robert's office.

PATRIZIA. Repeating the puddle scene with a different, international background means both continuity and growth.

ROBERT. Repeating the puddle scene means standstill, stagnation. No matter what the background is. But the market is booming, Patrizia. The market is booming. Those that stop are overtaken. Repeating the puddle is lethal.

PATRIZIA. We're not standing still. We're going to New York.

ROBERT. Copying the puddle in New York doesn't make it any better.

Pause.

PATRIZIA. Why didn't you call?

ROBERT. What?

Short pause.

PATRIZIA. Why didn't you call?

Pause.

ROBERT *bitter.* You're not serious –
Why should I have?

Pause.

PATRIZIA. The success of the first puddle ad bears me out – it's what people want. People loved the first puddle ad.

Pause.

ROBERT. That's not what this is about.

Short pause.

Why didn't you call?

PATRIZIA. It –

Short pause.

It –

ROBERT. I –

Short pause.

People want progress. People want the future and not a copy of yesterday's idea.

PATRIZIA. The puddle is not a copy.

ROBERT. This is about progress. People don't care about anything else.

Short pause.

PATRIZIA. Let's go somewhere and –

ROBERT. What?

Short pause.

PATRIZIA. Let's just go somewhere and have a drink and –

ROBERT. Why –

PATRIZIA. Let's go and have a drink and I'll tell you the difference between a copy and a quotation.

Short pause.

ROBERT. Aha.

PATRIZIA. And you'll tell me why you dislike New York.

Short pause.

ROBERT. We don't have to go anywhere for that. We can do that here.

Short pause.

PATRIZIA. True.

ROBERT. What?

PATRIZIA. We can do that here.

Pause.

I guess we should fuck each other right here, right now.

Short pause.

It would probably solve most of our problems.

Pause. They look at each other. Finally:

ROBERT. Maybe.

Pause.

But it wouldn't make your ad any better.

Pause.

PATRIZIA. As you like.

ROBERT. That's the way it is.

PATRIZIA. Just as you like.

Pause.

ROBERT. You want to tell me the difference between a copy and a quotation? In some bar, over a glass of wine? That's not necessary. You're quoting yourself, I got that much.

Short pause.

You're making a statement with your work. You're making a company statement. If you do the same thing as last year, then you're stating standstill. Apathy. And no one's interested in that.

Short pause.

That's not enough. I mean – don't forget: no matter where you want your career to go: you can't avoid doing some work. The puddle thing is probably the only idea you've ever had –

Short pause.

PATRIZIA. Enough now, careful –

ROBERT. Although – you know I wouldn't be surprised – : you probably stole the whole puddle idea from somewhere – is that possible?

Short pause.

Is that true? Correct? Have I guessed right?

Short pause. They look at each other.

PATRIZIA. This is it.

Short pause. She gets up.

This really is it.

ROBERT. This paper is old and it's rubbish.

He throws the paper in the bin.

PATRIZIA. We'll see about that.

2.9.

ROBERT. She left.

Short pause.

I took my time. I didn't care if she was going to get to Kramer first – because I knew that's what she was going to do. I was completely sure of myself: she didn't stand a chance.

I took the paper from the bin and reread it. I leaned back and waited. I looked out the window and slowly counted to a hundred. Maybe I was hoping something was going to happen. Maybe she was right: maybe Central Park was a good idea after all.

Short pause.

Then I took the paper and went to the lift to go up to Kramer, but then decided to take the stairs.

Short pause.

I paused in front of Kramer's door on the sixteenth floor for a moment. I stood there, in the corridor, and heard the keyboards clicking softly in the antechambers and the muffled voices speaking on the phone. I love the noises on the sixteenth floor, everything up there sounds different, even the daylight seems different there. I was nervous, but confident at the same time. Every time I'm on the sixteenth floor I get this feeling in my stomach – something like: this is where I want to get to.

Short pause.

I stood in front of Kramer's office and I thought of all the people that hadn't made it. That wanted to get up here just like me, up to the executive floor, and who some day got stuck. They made a mistake somewhere and fell by the wayside. While I went past them and was on my way.

Short pause.

Maybe Kramer wasn't even there – maybe he was busy.

Short pause.

Kramer was a little surprised to see me. I had expected to see her there, but she wasn't there yet. He read the paper perching on the edge of the desk on which we had –

Short pause.

I told him I didn't believe in the ad. That it would be a mistake to produce the puddle a second time. Financially, but most of all artistically. The first puddle ad was a huge success, yes, but the New York copy of the puddle would be a fiasco. The New York puddle would be an unmistakable signal of stagnation and consequently an obvious, predictable disaster.

I told him that Patrizia obviously doesn't understand what this is about. What's at stake here. And that therefore I wasn't interested in working with her in the future.

Short pause.

And I told him that the whole idea with the puddle was probably nicked from somewhere.

Short pause.

While I was talking Kramer mostly looked out the window, as usual when he was about to make a difficult decision. But then, when I had finished, he looked at me. He looked at me in a way he'd never looked at me before. He looked me in the eye and although he didn't say anything and just nodded, I felt like at that moment something in him broke.

Short pause.

When I left Kramer's office, she was walking along the corridor, towards me. That was the last time I saw her.

PATRIZIA. I walked out the office. I took my time. I didn't care if he was going to get to Kramer first – because I knew that's what he was planning to do. But I was completely sure of myself: he didn't stand a chance.

I went downstairs to my office and printed the paper again. I re-read it. I sat down behind my desk and waited. I looked out the window and slowly counted to a hundred. Maybe I was hoping something would happen. Maybe he was right: maybe Central Park wasn't a good idea after all.

And then I picked up the receiver and made an appointment with Kramer to present my new outline.

Come on up, he said, in about ten minutes.

I was nervous, but confident at the same time. Every time I'm on the sixteenth floor I get this feeling in my stomach – something like: this is where I want to get to.

They're clichés, yes, but one day I want to have my own d
in one of these offices. I want a large apartment – preferabl
in New York. I want to meet a good-looking man who carri
me across a huge puddle on a rainy day in Central Park,
because sometimes there are moments when you need help. I
want a child, and I want to sleep in my pyjamas at night, and
in the morning, after a chaotic taxi ride, I want to get out of
the car in a perfect suit with a hairstyle that's spontaneous but
great and get in the lift and come up here. I want to walk to
my office along the silent carpet and hear keyboards clicking
softly through the open doors of the antechambers.

Short pause.

Robert was just leaving Kramer's office. That was the last
time I saw him.

Short pause.

Kramer wasn't as surprised by the paper as I had expected –
Robert had just shown it to him. But he thought the idea to
re-shoot the puddle ad in New York was excellent. Central
Park. The light. The skyline. He was completely enthusiastic
– he was delighted. He talked about 'expansive continuity'.
He thought the idea was charming. *Let's go to New York*, he
said. *Patsy, let's go to New York.*

C.

Indian music. MARIA *in front of her locker. She opens it. Early
morning. It's 5.50 a.m. She puts down her bag. She pulls off her
winter boots, puts her coat, blouse and skirt in the locker. She's
in a hurry – like every morning. She takes her uniform and more
comfortable shoes out of the locker and gets dressed.*

3.

HANS *and* FRANK *are sitting across from each other.* HANS *is
sitting behind his desk.* HANS *is about sixty,* FRANK *about
thirty.*

HANS. Delhi –

Short pause.

I mean: Delhi. Just that word. That name. And how tangible it suddenly all is. Isn't it?

Short pause.

Right?

So close. Fantastic. Don't you think?

FRANK. Yes, yes.

HANS. No, seriously: what –

Short pause.

What do you think about when you hear that name? Delhi?

Short pause.

You – you don't have to tell me if you don't want to.

Short pause.

You don't have to.

FRANK. Well it's obvious.

Short pause.

I think about India. About the city.

Short pause.

About our office.

HANS. Stop.

FRANK. Hm?

HANS. Stop.

Short pause.

Be honest. And precise.

FRANK. Why?

HANS. You don't think about our office. You think about being in charge of the office.

Short pause.

FRANK. That too, yes.

HANS. Just wanted to clarify that.

Pause.

Just wanted to clarify that.

Pause.

FRANK. What do you think about?

HANS. When?

FRANK. When you hear Delhi.

HANS. About Kramer. First of all I think about Kramer, of course.

Pause.

FRANK. Okay. And then?

HANS. And then –

Short pause.

Then I think about a plane.

FRANK. Aha. –

Short pause.

HANS. I've learned through experience that it's better to visualise things if you want them to come true. You have to visualise them.

Short pause.

That's why I think about the plane.

FRANK. Sure.

Short pause.

About the plane. About what kind of plane?

HANS. I think about a large plane. Because it takes me there. About a Boeing.

FRANK. I surf a lot. I surf almost every night.

Short pause.

HANS. Because a plane is going to take me to Delhi. Away from here.

Great bird, take me to Delhi:
Take me to the Indian subcontinent.

FRANK. And I keep putting on weight. In the last ten years I've gained ten kilos. Ever since I started working here I keep getting fatter.

HANS. An eleven-hour non-stop flight landing in New Delhi, Indira Gandhi International Airport.

FRANK. Ten kilos in ten years. That means twenty kilos in twenty years and so on. But maybe it's an exponential curve. That would mean that at forty I'll be fifteen kilos heavier. And that between forty and fifty I'm going to put on twenty kilos. And so on. At sixty I would weigh 120 kilos. 120 kilos. That's almost one and a half tons.

Pause.

HANS. Do you work out?

Short pause.

FRANK. Why do you ask?

HANS. No, you don't work out.

Short pause.

Right?

Short pause.

No answer. No. But you should. Keeps you fresh in the head, too. It's good for your visual imagination. Apart from the body. From your body.

FRANK. I surf every night. On the way home from work I get a take-away pizza and a couple of beers. I come home and turn on the computer.

Short pause.

I do a couple of rounds on the flight simulator and with one hand I eat the slowly cooling pizza. When I was twenty-seven I had a steady girlfriend. Since she left I'm more or less alone. At about ten o'clock I open the second beer and go online.

HANS. In Delhi the humidity is often over 98 percent. It gets hot there. Up to fifty degrees. The heat shimmers on the street. Imagine you're there: imagine you work there: you need to be fit. You need to be in optimum physical shape. Otherwise you won't make it. Otherwise they'll fly you home after four weeks. Wouldn't be the first time.

FRANK. And you? Do you work out?

HANS. Every day.

Short pause.

FRANK. On the net your sense of time keeps changing. It still does.

Short pause.

I'd never pay extra for internet pictures. There are plenty of good webpages with free pictures. Thousands of free pictures.

Pause.

As soon as I'm online, I get hungry.

HANS. I keep getting thinner. I'm constantly losing weight. I'm in my early sixties now. Only a couple of years ago I was really fat. Heavy. Too much yellow fat on my hips. I could never control my weight. I just ate too much – I always had something in the early morning and then I had breakfast again in the canteen. Two hot meals a day: at noon and in the evening. And in between, snacks at work: Chocolate. Nuts. Crisps. Beer and wine in the evening. Hardly any sport. Every ten years I was ten kilos heavier. At thirty I weighed seventy kilos, at forty eighty, at fifty ninety. More and more.

But now – I have regular check-ups. I'm okay. My doctor's happy with me.

My daughter isn't. 'If this continues, daddy,' she says, 'I'll take that thing away again.' 'That thing' was a present from her – a year and a half ago. Because I don't get enough exercise – before the heart gives out.

That thing is a home trainer. One of those bikes you put in your room to ride in one place.

FRANK. As soon as I'm online I get hungry. That's the problem.

HANS. The home trainer is in my living room, in the same spot where the three-seater used to be. When I work out I either look out through the big windows and into the garden, or I look at the TV and the stereo. My wife used to take care of the garden, now it's slowly becoming dilapidated. Slowly becoming overgrown. Doesn't matter. Bothers the neighbours – well, so what.

FRANK. Chocolate. Nuts. Crisps.

HANS. My daughter and I moved the three-seater to the basement. I don't get many visitors nowadays.

When I come home I've already eaten. I eat somewhere along the way, in town. A salad. Not much. Something with tofu. I rarely cook at home. Or go out for a proper meal. I wouldn't know who to take. I come home and I get changed. I make myself a cup of tea. And then I get on the home trainer and

start to work out. Now my weekday routine takes up to four
hours. I couldn't manage that much before. I've improved. I
start slowly and then I gradually increase the speed. In the
beginning I had problems with my knees, but that passed. In
the evenings I do between eighty and a hundred kilometres.
Next to the home trainer there's a road map with the
distances marked up so I can see how much I'm doing.

Short pause.

Or I play videotapes of a Tour de France stage race. I've done
whole stage races on my bike – of course not in the evenings,
you can't do that – but at the weekends. Of course I can't
keep up – but nonetheless I'm in good shape – for my age.
There are a lot of boys I could overtake. I'm in my early
sixties now – I could have another twenty or thirty years
ahead of me. Twenty or thirty years: lots of time. Lots of
time.

Pause.

I just wonder what's ahead for me.

Short pause.

What I'm working out for. What I'm really doing it for.

Short pause.

FRANK. I'm only interested in the hard stuff. I'm not interested
in teenagers. I particularly like the Italian, the Hungarian and
the French freepic-pages. Megasalope alone has hundreds of
pictures. Hundreds of women. The pictures are authentic,
they're real, the women in the photos are really doing it, but
they don't have names, they just have numbers. But I give
them names anyway. And while I look at Natascha, Suzie or
Julia, I forget the commands, the numbers, the programming
systems. I stop thinking about it.

Short pause.

I sit in front of the computer and wonder where Suzie on
megasalope is really from. Where these pictures were taken:
in France or in Hungary or in America. Or in Germany, Italy
or Russia. Where did she strip for the camera? Maybe she
lives just round the corner. Where is the man she's having sex
with on the photos? Who's the photographer? Does she
always do this? Or did she just do it this one time. How much
did she get for it, if she got anything for it? How old is the
photo? Where is she now? Where is she now, while I'm

sitting here? What's she doing at this moment while I'm looking at her photo? Is she thinking about this? Is she thinking about the fact that maybe someone is looking at her right now?

Or take Natascha – One night her photos just disappeared, the whole webpage suddenly looks different. It's been updated. Natascha is gone. Maybe there are still some pictures of her on the web – but where? I search through the servers at night but I can't find her. I've never found the same woman on two different sites. The pictures are interchangeable, but Natascha is in none of them. Maybe she doesn't even exist any more. I search for her on the world wide web but I can't find her. And all this still takes so long.

Pause.

In the end, around one o'clock, I turn off the computer. I sit there, with my mouth open, and I feel the air dropping into my lungs. For a moment my head is empty.

Music.

And then the numbers reappear, and the commands, the programme steps, and I wonder how you could make it faster, more complex and better: The information highways, the servers, the processors, the programmes.

Short pause.

And that's why I'm the right man for Delhi.

Pause.

HANS. I know you applied for the Delhi job.

FRANK. I see.

Pause.

HANS. And of course you know I applied. Of course you know. I mean – after all you work for me.

FRANK. Oh really?

HANS. For me, yes. Or for my team. Or my department. Or for the company. For Kramer. Anyway. At least you do at the moment.

Short pause.

But what's to become of that. I mean – suppose you get the Delhi job – and I don't. You get on the plane to India while

I stay here? So I get kicked out in the autumn, in the next company restructure? After twenty-five years?

Short pause.

Because I don't suppose you intend to take me to Delhi with you. Correct? You're not stupid. But can you really imagine that? Me taking early retirement?

Short pause.

I can't. I mean, I can't imagine that – just so you can work out your prospects.

Short pause.

But it's nice that you're trying. To be a good sport. Doesn't suit you.

Short pause.

But I still think we have to get something clear here.

FRANK. Aha.

HANS. Yes.

Short pause.

I think there's an important point you haven't grasped yet.

FRANK. Yes?

HANS. Visual imagination.

FRANK. Exactly. Visual imagination. Your speciality.

HANS. Correct. Visual and spatial imagination.

FRANK. And?

HANS. And what?

FRANK. You said there was an important point I hadn't grasped. I'd like to know what point that is.

Short pause.

Really.

HANS. Oh yes, correct: you –

Short pause

How far is the wall behind you? What would you say?

Short pause.

FRANK. The wall –

HANS. Yes, the wall. How far is it?

Pause. Frank shrugs.

It's really a very simple question, isn't it? You can see the desk, me, the shelf behind me and the wall. How many metres do you think until the wall blocks your sight? What would you say?

FRANK. No idea.

HANS *with flash of anger.* Why doesn't that interest you, why are you so vague?

FRANK. Okay, three metres.

HANS. Three metres? Two and a half. At the most.

FRANK. Alright, two and a half, so?

HANS. Two and a half metres to the wall. That's your field of vision.

Short pause.

And now try to imagine what I see.

Short pause.

Because my point of view is quite different.

Short pause.

I can't see the wall at all. I can see the front edge of my desk, you behind it, and behind you, maybe four metres away, the entrance to my office.

FRANK. And?

HANS. You see: it's something quite different – I mean – we're in the same room but we see completely different things. We don't share the same picture.

FRANK. I'm not interested. Maybe you'll get to the point now.

HANS. Maybe you'd like to take a look? Come on over. We can trade places for a minute.

FRANK. Thank you, that's not necessary.

HANS. Not necessary. So you think you can imagine it like that.

Short pause.

What – this – looks like from my perspective.

Short pause.

Possible. Maybe.

Short pause.

I don't think so. I think you lack the imagination that's required. The faculty of imagination.

FRANK. I can handle it, don't worry.

HANS. And that's why you don't have the drive that's required.

Short pause.

FRANK. Depends on what for, I'd say.

HANS. What for?

Short pause.

For Delhi. I mean the drive that's required for Delhi. What did you think?

Short pause.

I mean: what if I get the job. Not you. It's possible. What are you going to do then? I can hardly take you with me if you wouldn't have taken me.

FRANK. When I applied I was sure I was going to get the job. It's simple.

Pause.

HANS. Yes, yes. How long have you been with us?

FRANK. You know that better than me.

HANS. Aha. Right.

Short pause.

I thought we could have a conversation.

FRANK. I wouldn't know what about.

HANS. It's simple: I ask you a question, you give me an answer. I ask you how long you've worked here, and you say – for example – six years. And then I can say: how quickly time passes. Six years ago I gave you a job, I was your mentor for six years and now you want to take my job. But that's not going to happen.

Short pause.

FRANK. Yes it will –

HANS. You're sure? It's been six years and you keep getting fatter.

Short pause.

Right?

FRANK. You –

HANS. Is it possible? Is it possible that you're getting fatter every year? I mean: what if this carries on: it's not a nice thought.

Pause.

And that's why we're going to have dinner together now.

Short pause.

Do you know that little Italian place round the corner? Or would you rather go someplace else? I don't care as long as they have good wine. For our farewell.

FRANK. What farewell?

HANS. I knew that was going to arouse your curiosity. A farewell dinner. At last: some show of interest.

FRANK. What farewell do you mean?

Short pause.

HANS. I've got reliable information that I'm at the top of Kramer's list.

FRANK. What list –

HANS. The list for –

Short pause.

Oh come on Frank, you know.

FRANK. No, no idea, what list are you on?

Pause.

HANS. The list. The list for Delhi. I'm to take over Delhi.

Pause.

FRANK. I see –

HANS. Yes – and I think we should celebrate that, shouldn't we?

Short pause.

FRANK. Who told you that?

HANS. What?

FRANK. That you're at the top of Kramer's list, who told you that? Kramer didn't tell you that.

HANS. Why – no, someone close to Kramer told me.

Short pause.

FRANK. Aha.

HANS. But the information is one hundred per cent correct,
absolutely reliable, don't worry. I'm expecting a phonecall
from Kramer any minute now.

Pause.

I can picture it now: the two of us in a restaurant. Despite
everything. I don't carry grudges. After our chat in the lift
down to the lobby – it was a long day – we go straight to
Maurizio, a good little Italian just round the corner. The table
is booked for half past eight. Not one of the tables at the front
but at the back, where it's more quiet. No mineral water
today but champagne, Maurizio knows that. Oysters, then a
simple minestrone, antipasti, spaghetti with aubergines,
tomatoes and pine kernels, then an ostrich steak and flan for
desert. And a gorgeous barolo to go with it – it's been ages
since I drank a really good wine. It's been ages since I've had
such a good meal. No one cares that we're not dressed
properly, this place is too discreet for that, and I'm a good
customer – or at least I used to be – with my wife. When
there was something to celebrate. Like today. And so the
evening passes in a flash – we're both laughing about the
whole thing, and we're talking:

About our weight, different workouts. About the Tour de
France.

FRANK. Sometimes I wish I could talk to Natascha. I mean: for
real. Really talk.

Short pause.

HANS. Gone midnight already, it's getting late, an espresso just
this once and a grappa on the house. What a lovely evening.

Pause.

FRANK. The problem is, Hans, your information is wrong.
What they told you isn't true.

HANS. Oh yes?

FRANK. Yes.

Short pause.

You're not going to take over Delhi.

Pause.

I'm going to take over Delhi.

Pause

I'm going to stroll along sunny streets smelling of saffron. I'm going to stroll from the research centre to my house. Everything is in full bloom, it's purple and white. There are coloured birds living in the trees, and little monkeys. There's an elephant grazing in the garden.

I'm sitting at my desk on the first floor of my house and I look out the window. I don't surf as much as I used to but I think I've found Natascha – on a Czech webpage. Of course I'm not completely sure. You can never be sure.

HANS. Who says?

FRANK. Kramer says.

HANS. Kramer –

Short pause.

FRANK. Kramer has given me the Delhi job.

HANS. That's not possible.

FRANK. It is.

Pause.

HANS. How long have you known?

Short pause.

FRANK. Three days.

Short pause.

HANS. Three days. That long –

Short pause.

Why didn't you tell me before? Why didn't Kramer let me know?

Pause.

Why didn't Kramer tell me?

Short pause.

I only saw him yesterday.

Pause. FRANK *in particular is quiet.*

FRANK. Of course we have dinner. I wouldn't know who else to take. We celebrate. But the bill's on me. We go to Benjarong, that Thai restaurant. I sometimes get a takeaway from Benjarong, I like the woman at the counter. We sit by the window and look at the street. He has vegetable soup, I take the wonton soup, order spring rolls for both of us, but he doesn't touch his. Afterwards I have meat with peanuts and rice and he has fried tofu.

HANS. In India they burn their dead by the roadside. Apparently when a man dies often his widow kills herself as well. But not the other way round. The men are left over.

FRANK. And we talk. About the internet. About weight. About working out. About India.

HANS. My daughter says I should do more in the evenings and at the weekends. Go out, see people. She says otherwise she'll take away my bike.

Laughs a little. Short pause.

When I've finished working out I check in the kitchen if I've turned off the cooker, then I turn off the lights in the kitchen and in the living room. I check if I've locked the front door, turn off the light in the hallway, run up the stairs to the first floor, turn off the light on the landing, have a quick shower, brush my teeth and go to bed in our former bedroom.

The house is too big for me but I'm not ready to say goodbye to all this.

I lie in bed. It's one o'clock. I can feel the air falling into my lungs. I think about my home trainer. If I should have it serviced.

Short pause.

And then I wonder if I turned the cooker off – downstairs in the kitchen.

Pause.

I get up again. I turn on the light on the landing and run downstairs. And I check the cooker. It was off. I recheck the front door. I run back to the kitchen to check if I turned off the kitchen light after I checked the cooker – and at the same time I glance at the hotplate. Off.

Then I climb up the stairs again but I turn back halfway up, run downstairs and try the front door again. Locked. The light

outside the front door is off. The light in the hallway is off.
The light in the living room is off. The cooker is turned off.

Short pause.

Or is it?

Short pause.

And what about the light in the basement. Didn't I go down
the basement earlier? Was that today? The light in the
basement is off. The door to the basement is locked. I climb
back up the stairs and go to bed. Turn the light off. Is the
light on the landing still on? I get up again and check if
I turned off the light on the landing. It's off. – Everything's
locked. Everything's turned off.

FRANK. How are you doing?

Short pause.

HANS. Have you got a girlfriend?

That's nice for you.

What's her name?

Short pause.

That's nice. Sounds Russian. That's a nice, rare name.

FRANK. Great bird, take me to Delhi:

Take me to Madras, to Bangalore,

take me to the east, to the morning, in the night,

take me to the Indian subcontinent.

D.

MARIA. I work for a big corporation. In the so-called mother-
ship, the company's head office – it's a skyscraper. I work on
the groundfloor, in the lobby, in the control room. Everyone
that enters or leaves the building walks past us. People look
funny when they rush past you in the morning. Especially the
women, when they come in here just after nine and they're
in a real hurry.

My early shift starts three hours earlier, at six. I'm one of
those people that sit on the tram at 5.40 a.m. Nonetheless

I like the early shift best. The night shift is worst. On the night shift we also have to do the round through the building, and then I'm scared. We have to check every room and every office, and I always think that one night we're going to find someone that hanged himself after work. It's possible. Some guy. A few years away from retirement. It has happened. When I arrive for the early shift usually my colleague Heinrich is already there. He's already put on his uniform and unwrapped his sandwiches. And he's turned on the little TV he's sneaked in next to the other monitors. Between six and seven in the morning nothing happens except for the cleaning ladies slowly leaving the building – and that's why Heinrich and I usually watch TV together at that time.

Our company even has an ad. Heinrich doesn't particularly like the ad but I do. I don't understand the connection between the ad and our company, but it doesn't matter. Now there's even a new ad, although it's basically like the old one – but the new ad is set in New York, in Central Park. You can see the skyline.

A woman is standing in Central Park, in front of a huge puddle. She can't walk over it in her court shoes, and then a good-looking guy helps her. He just carries her, he takes her and carries her over the puddle – the way you'd carry a bride across the threshold. Heinrich doesn't like it. Heinrich wants more action, but I like it. I think it's romantic. Sure – the whole thing is nicked – it's from that film with Michelle Pfeiffer and George Clooney, but – who cares. I mean – it doesn't matter.

Heinrich always says 'but it's not like that, it would never happen in real life.' And then he looks at me and says 'right, right, Maria, just look at you and me. I don't carry you across any puddles either.' And then I imagine what it would look like if Heinrich carried me over a puddle: that makes me laugh. Always. Almost every morning.